All Kinds of Homes

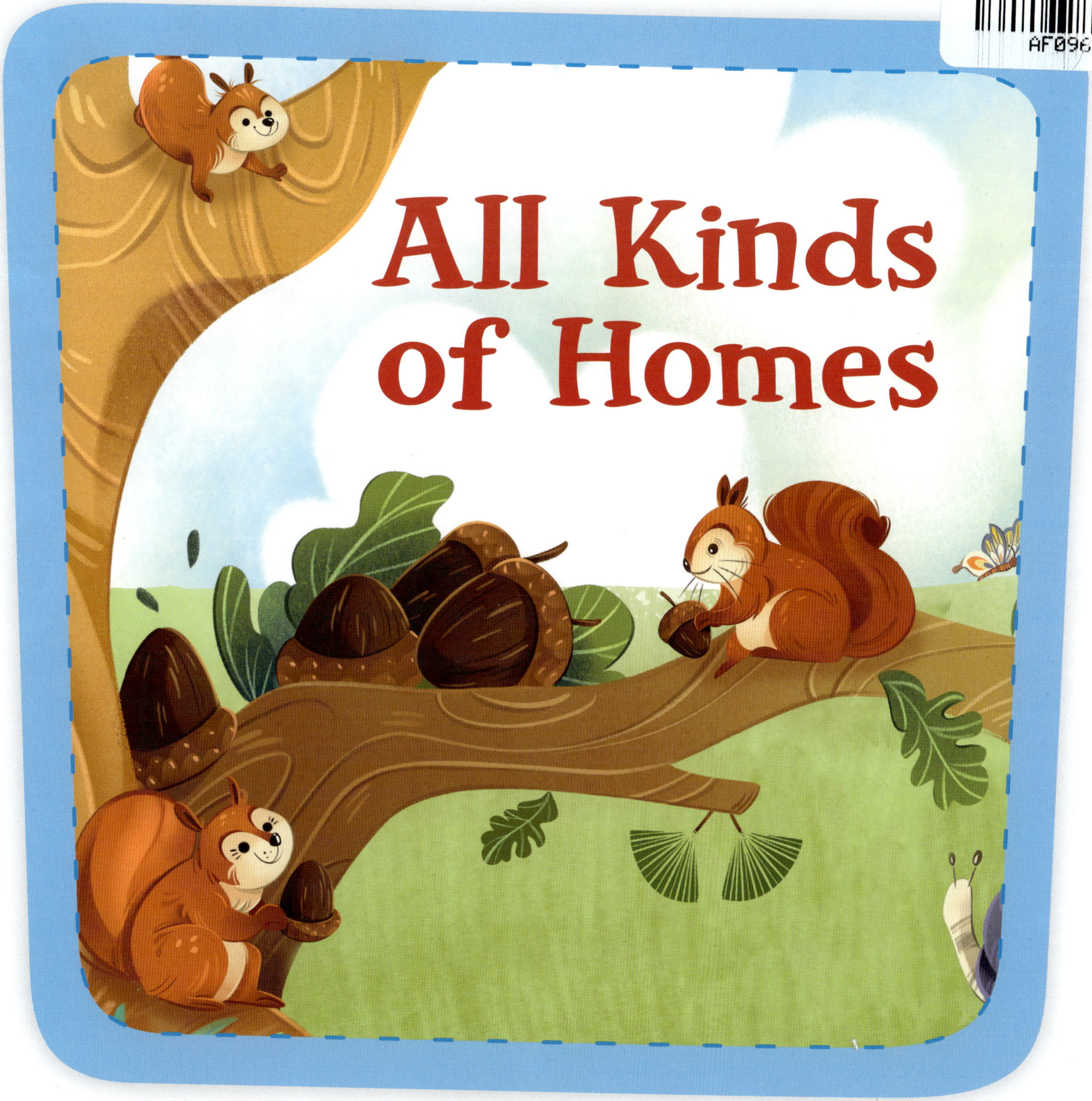

Dona Herweck Rice

Illustrated by Emanuela Di Donna

Some squirrels live inside their trees.

Honey hives are for the bees.

Beavers lodge nearby their dams

Barns are good for sheep and lambs.

Burrows are a place for mice.

Bats agree their caves are nice.

Lions live within the brush.

Meerkats think their plains are lush.

Dolphins dwell within the sea.

But there are many homes for you and me!

Notes for the Grown-ups

This book allows for a rich shared reading experience for children who are early and developing readers. The rhyme and images help new readers to tell the story, either as they read or as they are read to. What a valuable tool for building the confidence new readers need to embark on the adventures that await them while reading!

To extend this reading experience, do one or more of the following:

- After reading, come back to the book again and again. Rereading is an excellent tool for building literacy skills.

- Ask the child to draw more pages for the book, showing different types of animals in their homes.

- Consider together why humans live in so many different types of homes.

- Name all the types of homes shown in the book.

- Discuss what it might be like if a human lived in an animal home, and what it might be like if an animal lived in a human home.

Consultant

Cynthia Malo, M.A.Ed.

Publishing Credits

Rachelle Cracchiolo, M.S.Ed., *Publisher*
Emily R. Smith, M.A.Ed., *SVP of Content Development*
Véronique Bos, *VP of Creative*
Dona Herweck Rice, *Senior Content Manager*
Fabiola Sepulveda, *Art Director*

Library of Congress Cataloging in Publication Control Number:
2024007564

This book may not be reproduced or distributed in any way without prior written consent from the publisher.

5482 Argosy Avenue
Huntington Beach, CA 92649
www.tcmpub.com
ISBN 979-8-7659-6129-2
© 2025 Teacher Created Materials, Inc.
Printed by: 926. Printed in: Malaysia. PO#: PO11723